诸子百家国风画传

Biographies of Great Thinkers

孟子

画传

图／李维定
文／路艳艳
译／秦悦

# MENCIUS

济南出版社

图书在版编目（CIP）数据

孟子画传 / 李维定著 . —— 济南 ：济南出版社 ,2014.12（诸子百家国风画传）（2017.4 重印）
ISBN 978-7-5488-1377-4

Ⅰ . ①孟… Ⅱ . ①李… Ⅲ . ①孟轲（前 390 ～前 305）－传记－画册 Ⅳ . ① B222.5-64

中国版本图书馆 CIP 数据核字 (2014) 第 290916 号

◆图 / 李维定　◆文 / 路艳艳　◆译 / 秦悦

◎“原动力”中国原创动漫出版扶持计划入选项目
◎上海市重大文艺创作项目由上海文化发展基金会资助
◎上海市文化“走出去”项目由上海市文化“走出去”专项扶持资金赞助

## 孟子画传

| | |
|---|---|
| 出版发行 | 济南出版社 |
| 总 执 行 | 上海海派连环画中心 |
| | 上海城市动漫出版传媒有限公司 |
| | 济南出版有限责任公司 |
| 项目策划 | 刘　军　刘亚军 |
| 出版策划 | 崔　刚　朱孔宝 |
| 出版执行 | 张承军 |
| 责任编辑 | 王小曼　张雪丽 |
| 特约编辑 | 刘蓉蓉　孙羽翎　余　阳　董广印 |
| 装帧设计 | 舒晓春　焦萍萍 |

| | |
|---|---|
| 印　　刷 | 济南鲁艺彩印有限公司 |
| 开　　本 | 210mm×285mm　　16 开 |
| 印　　张 | 5.75 |
| 字　　数 | 90 千 |
| 版　　次 | 2014 年 12 月第 1 版 |
| 印　　次 | 2017 年 4 月第 2 次印刷 |
| 标准书号 | ISBN 978-7-5488-1377-4 |
| 定　　价 | 45.00 元 |

# 前言

2014年3月，中国国家主席习近平在联合国教科文组织总部的演讲中指出：「中华文明经历了五千多年的历史变迁，但始终一脉相承，积淀着中华民族最深层的精神追求，代表着中华民族独特的精神标识，为中华民族生生不息、发展壮大提供了丰厚滋养。」中华传统文化是涓涓流水，润物无声，滋养了世代中国人的精神家园。在中华传统文化波澜壮阔的历史画卷中，诸子百家文化就是其中浓墨重彩的一页。

充满先贤智慧的诸子百家文化，是集中华传统文化、哲学、艺术于一体的文明宝藏：反对暴力，期盼人与人之间和睦相处、以礼相待，这是儒家思想的『仁』；平等博爱，止息不义战争，这是墨家思想的『兼爱非攻』；遵循自然、万物和谐，这是道家思想的『道法自然』；论兵却主张『不战而屈人之兵』，这是充满智慧光芒的兵家思想……诸子百家的思想，正包含着人们所努力构造的幸福世界中的重要基石。这是中华民族的财富，也是世界文明的重要组成部分。

近代以来，上海作为中华文明走向世界的一个重要窗口，担当着向世界展示中国文化华彩精粹的重要使命。建设充满活力的国际文化大都市，上海更需要放眼全球、放眼全国，以『海纳百川』的精神打造中华文化精品，推动中华文化走向世界。

这套由国务院新闻办公室支持，上海市政府新闻办公室协力出版的《诸子百家国风画传》丛书，化繁难为轻逸、化艰深为平易，充满了思想美、故事美、人性美、艺术美。它将诸子思想中的妙笔华章与国画家的水墨丹青巧妙结合，书香墨趣将诸子的音容笑貌、神采风骨生动地呈现在读者面前。它向世界打开了中华传统文化之门，同时也为中华文化拓展国际文化交流，进行了新的尝试和创新，提供了新的载体和通道。

诸子百家文化精神正如追逐理性、自由与美的古希腊人文精神一般，是人类共同的文化财富。希望诸位读者从这套书出发，分享故事，体验艺术，感悟哲理，开始一段美不胜收的中华传统文化探源之旅。

二○一四年九月

# Preface

In March of 2014, President Xi Jinping pointed out in his speech delivered in the headquarters of UNESCO, "Having gone through over 5000 years of vicissitudes, the Chinese civilization has always kept to its original root. Unique in representing China spiritually, it contains some most profound pursuits of the Chinese nation and provides it with abundant nourishment for existence and development." The Chinese traditional culture is just like trickling water irrigating and nurturing the spiritual realm of Chinese people. In the long and splendid picture of Chinese cultural history, the contributions of great thinkers are the most glorious chapter.

The wisdom and philosophies of these great thinkers crystallized culture, philosophy and art in our Chinese civilization: Confucian "benevolence", Mohist "universal love", Taoist "modeling itself after Nature" and the military teaching about "attaining victory in war without fighting" are still holding the stage. These fascinating thoughts constitute the cornerstones of an ideal world that Chinese people dream of having. These spiritual assets not only belong to Chinese people but also constitute an integral part of the world civilization.

As an important window in modern times, Shanghai has assumed a mission to demonstrate the brilliance of Chinese culture. To construct a dynamic international cultural metropolis and to promote Chinese culture to the world, Shanghai needs a mind so open to the entire country and entire world and a mind so tolerant as the vast ocean admitting hundreds of rivers.

*The Pictorial Biographies of Great Thinkers* supported by The State Council Information Office and Information Office of Shanghai Municipality is a close cooperation between Information Office of Shandong Provincial People's Government and Information Office of Henan Provincial People's Government. This series in Chinese painting style simplified the complicated history into simple stories, revealing the beauty of human nature as well as artistic creation. The ink painting presented vividly the personalities of great thinkers, attracting readers to explore their great thoughts and ideas. The pictorial biographies helped open the door of Chinese traditional culture to the world, and this attempt also provided a new carrier and channel for cultural exchange.

The brilliant Chinese culture is fascinating. Like the pursuit for reason, freedom and beauty in ancient Greek humanism, the legacy from these great thinkers is also the cultural assets shared by the whole humanity. It is hoped that readers can embark on a journey to explore traditional Chinese culture through reading these books.

September 2014

孟子画传
MENCIUS

# 编者的话

孟子是战国时期儒家的代表人物，后世尊其为『亚圣』。他提出的民本思想和仁政学说影响深远。《孟子画传》以孟子的人生经历为轨迹，从『孟母三迁』至最后隐世著述，详细地描绘了孟子的日常生活、讲学游历。文中关于孟子对亲人、朋友、弟子的感情大量着墨，使读者对孟子有更直观、更亲切的认识。国画家李维定在对孟子进行绘画演绎时，以线条的运用来支撑整个画面，用色古朴典雅，韵味十足，这既与孟子不卑不亢的人生姿态相呼应，又展现了传统国画中海派人物画的独特魅力。画家十分注重图画对文字的拓展，画中人物表情丰富、动作鲜明，让读者仿佛置身于孟子的身旁，体味这位古代哲人的丰富人生历程，感受其思想的博大精深。

# Editor's Note

Mencius, who was called a sage next only to Confucius, is one of the representing figures of Confucian school during the Warring States Period. The people-based thought and benevolent governing he proposed have a far-reaching impact. *Mencius* traces his life from his mother's three relocation for his better education to his writing in seclusion, describing in detail his daily life and his lecture tours. *Mencius* highlights his affection for his family, his friends and his disciples, making the sage so approachable to us. In representing Mencius, the artist Li Weiding uses lines to prop up the picture and a delightful color to dignify the character. The vivid painting completes the profound meaning that words can not convey, making Mencius, his life and philosophy more understandable to the readers.

# 目录

Contents

◎群雄争霸图
Warlords striving for hegemony

　　2400多年前，中华大地上分布着大大小小上百个诸侯国，除秦、楚、齐、燕、韩、赵、魏7个大国外，还有宋、鲁、郑、卫、蔡、薛、滕等诸多小国。200多年间，大国为了争夺土地、兼并小国，常常短兵相接、相互攻击，因此这个时代被人们称为"战国时代"。

　　"战国"还包含着另一层含义：诸子们唇枪舌剑，相互批判、辩论，出现了"百家争鸣"的局面。儒、墨、名、法、农、阴阳等各个学派为参与政治，争相阐述、发扬自己的思想与治国方略。

More than 2400 years ago, there were more than 100 states in China. Apart from the 7 biggest states—Qin, Chu, Qi, Yan, Han, Zhao and Wei, there were other smaller states such as Song, Lu, Zheng, Wei, Cai, Xue and Teng. For over 200 years, these states fought against each other for the acquisition of land and the ultimate leadership. This historical period is described as "the Warring States Period".

"The Warring States" has another layer of meaning: Great thinkers challenged each other's ideas. Their criticizing and debating ushered in an era characterized with different schools of thoughts contending for attention. Famous schools of thoughts such as Confucianism, Mohism, the Ming school studying the concept of objects and the relationship between object and name, the Legalist school, the Agriculturist school and the Yin-Yang school, all elaborated their own thoughts and argued for their understanding of statecraft.

◎孟轲诞生图

The birth of Mencius

　　周烈王四年（公元前372年）四月初二，这个动荡不安年代里的普通一天，邹国凫村中的孟氏一家却欢天喜地，经过十个月的煎熬与等待，他们终于迎来了一个可爱的男婴——孟轲（孟子）。虽然小孟轲尚在襁褓之中，但为了家计，即使有再多的不舍，孟父也不得不常年在外奔波，于是照顾、教养儿子的重任就落在了孟母一个人的身上。

In 372 B. C., the fourth year under King Lie of Zhou's reign, on an ordinary day of April in Chinese lunar calendar, Mencius was born into a family in Fu Village of the State of Zou. The Mengs was very happy to have this little boy after 10 months' expecting. Though Meng Ke (Mencius) was still in the cradle, his father had to say goodbye to him to earn a living elsewhere all the year round. Meng Ke's mother had to take good care of him and educate him on her own.

◎孟母三迁图

Mother moving residences for his better upbringing

　　孟家住在墓地旁边，每有葬礼，小孟轲就去凑热闹。母亲见他玩耍时总模仿葬礼仪式——挖坑、埋东西、跪拜、号哭，认为这不是他该学的东西，于是决定搬家。他们搬到商铺林立、热闹非常的集市旁。小孟轲又和新朋友玩起了做买卖的游戏，一会儿高声叫卖，一会儿讨价还价。孟母觉得这种环境也不利于孩子成长，便再次离开。这次，他们搬到学宫旁。学子们每日学习设俎豆祭祀祖先、揖让进退觐见诸侯的礼仪，小孟轲也时时模仿，孟母欣然定居于此。

孟府　又称亚圣府，位于山东邹城南
关，始建于北宋晚期，是孟子嫡系后
裔居住处，距今已有 800 余年历史。
孟府初建时规模较小，后经历代重修
扩建，至清初已形成前后 7 进院落。
以主体建筑"大堂"为界，前为官衙，
中为内宅，后为花园，共有楼、堂、亭、
阁 148 间，是国内规模宏大、保存较
为完整、较为典型的官衙与内宅合一
的古建筑群和地主庄园之一。

The Mengs lived quite near to a cemetery. Whenever there was a funeral, little Meng Ke would go along for the ride. His mother noticed that when he played games, he acted out what he had seen at a funeral — digging, burying, kneeling and wailing. Thinking this was not what Meng Ke was supposed to learn, his mother decided to move away. They moved to a place near a busy market. Little Meng Ke played with his friends the game of peddlers, selling and bargaining loudly. Mother thought this would do no good to him, either, and decided to move again. Finally, they settled down near a school. Students there learned rites of offering sacrifices and the etiquettes of presenting oneself to the dukes. Little Meng Ke often followed their examples to do the same. Mother settled down there gladly.

◎孟母断机图
Mother cutting off the fabric

　　为了供小孟轲读书，母亲省吃俭用，整日织布贴补家用。这天，小孟轲读完书后也不跟老师告别就匆匆回了家。孟母见他回来，便问道："学习进展到了什么程度？"小孟轲敷衍道："还和以前一样。"见儿子这样不求上进，孟母拿起剪刀，剪断了正在织的布。

　　小孟轲见状害怕极了，忙问母亲这样做的原因。孟母说："你荒废学业，就像我剪断这织布机（上的布）一样。织布，必须从一根根线开始，一寸一寸地织成一匹，然后才能做衣服。读书也是这个道理。学习不是一天两天的事，如果不能持之以恒，像你这样半途而废、浅尝辄止，以后怎能成才呢？"孟轲听了母亲的教诲后，早晚勤学，诵读经典。

　　Mother made a living by weaving and saved every penny possible for Meng Ke's schooling. One day, Meng Ke hurried home without saying goodbye to his teacher. Mother asked, "What have you learned today?" Meng Ke answered absent-mindedly, "The same as usual." Seeing that her son was not taking studies seriously, Mother cut off a piece of fabric she was weaving with a pair of scissors.

　　Meng Ke was frightened at this sight. He asked her what the matter was. Mother said, "You neglected your studies just like I cut the cloth on the loom. One must spin the yarn from the beginning before she weaved the cotton cloth inch by inch in order to make clothes. The same is true for studying. Learning calls for time. If a man does not learn or stop the work halfway, how is he able to be successful?" From then on, Meng Ke studied very hard, citing classics from dawn till dusk.

◎孟轲勤学图
Mencius studying hard

君子之泽，五世而斩；小人之泽，亦五世而斩。予未得为孔子徒也，予私淑诸人也。（《孟子·离娄下》）

　　十五六岁时，孟轲拜孔子的嫡孙子思的门人为师，学习儒家思想、孔子言论。吟诵着圣人之言，再对照当时的社会状况，孟轲更觉得各国诸侯急功近利，对内聚敛财富，对外互相侵伐，以至于生灵涂炭。苏秦、张仪之徒为诸侯出谋划策，助长了祸乱。当世之人没有值得仿效的，只有孔子提倡的才是正道。

　　When Meng Ke was about fifteen or sixteen years old, he studied Confucian thoughts under the supervision of a master who was the disciple of Confucius' grandson. He acquired the teachings of Confucius and reflected upon what the society was experiencing. He came to the realization that different dukedoms were all after quick success and instant benefits. They amassed wealth and launched wars, at the expense of their people living in great misery and suffering. Political strategists such as Su Qin and Zhang Yi's advice for the dukes only led to more disasters. No one was wiser than Confucius and nothing was worthy of learning from except what Confucius advocated.

◎孟子见邹穆公图
Mencius visiting Duke Mu of Zou

孟子曰："君子有三乐，而王天下不与存焉。父母俱存，
兄弟无故，一乐也。仰不愧于天，俯不怍于人，二乐也。
得天下英才而教育之，三乐也。"（《孟子·尽心上》）

　　三十而立，寒窗苦读十几载的孟轲终有所成。为了弘扬圣人学说，他开始授徒讲学，在教学相长的过程中形成了自己的思想体系和政治主张。他要改变这个衰乱之世，开启一个仁义社会、太平盛世。孟子的弟子越来越多，影响也越来越大。邹穆公听说后，征召孟子问询治国之道。于是，孟子去拜访穆公，向穆公陈述自己的政治主张。此时，他已经四十岁了。

　　It is believed that one should have established some kind of career when he turns 30. After years of hard work, Meng Ke achieved something. To advance and enrich the teachings of Confucius, he started to teach his own disciples. He developed his own philosophical thinking and political claims. He would change this chaotic world and usher in a harmonious and prosperous era. With more and more disciples following him, his influence was getting stronger and stronger. Duke Mu of Zou heard of him, and invited him to ask about the statecraft. Therefore, Mencius paid a visit to Duke Mu and stated his political views. At that time, he was 40 years old.

◎邹鲁交战图
Zou and Lu at war

孟子曰："民为贵，社稷次之，君为轻。是故得乎丘民而为天子，得乎天子为诸侯，得乎诸侯为大夫。"（《孟子·尽心下》）

　　邹国与鲁国发生冲突，邹国官员为守城牺牲，百姓却没人去帮忙营救，眼睁睁地看着他们死去。邹穆公非常生气，问孟子该如何处罚百姓。孟子劝慰说："灾荒之年，国君府库充盈，粮食满仓，百姓却四处逃命，饿死荒野，而官员却不把这些告诉您。遇到战争，百姓怎么会去救他们呢？只有平时对百姓仁爱，他们才会亲近官员，愿为官员牺牲。"

　　The State of Zou and the State of Lu were at war. Many officials of Zou died in defending the city, but the ordinary people just stood by and did not try to offer any help. Duke Mu of Zou was very angry. He asked Mencius about how to punish these people. Mencius said, "In a famine year, the treasury was overfilled, and the granary was also full, but the ordinary people had to flee from being starved to death. That's what the officials did not tell you. How can you expect them to save their officials when a war breaks out? Only if the officials love their people, can the people die for their superiors."

鼎 中国古代的一种青铜器,三足两耳,用来烹煮和盛贮肉类。相传夏禹铸九鼎象征九州,鼎因此成为传国重器,象征国家与权力。作为祭祀礼器,用鼎多少是身份的标志:"礼祭,天子九鼎,诸侯七,卿大夫五,元士三也"。

◎孟子游齐图
Mencius touring Qi

　　孟子在邹期间,仕途没有大进展,父亲也因病去世,经济拮据的他买了最普通的棺木,依士大夫礼制,用三个鼎供奉了牛、鱼、腊肉,安葬了父亲。为父守丧三年后,见自己的主张仍得不到重视,四十多岁的孟子怀揣"仁政"治国的抱负,率弟子离开父母之乡,远游他国,开始了长达二十多年的游历生涯。

　　早在齐桓公时期,齐国国都临淄就设有稷下学宫,邀请各派学者前来著书立说、议论政治。齐威王时,稷下学宫更为兴盛。于是,孟子把齐国作为自己游历的第一站。

　　Mencius did not make significant achievement in his political career in the State of Zou, and at that time his father died of sickness. Mencius was very poor and he could only afford a very ordinary coffin. He buried his father according to the rituals a scholar-official could practice: He offered in three vessels sacrifices of ox, fish and preserved meat. After three years of mourning for his father, he still could not see his political claim get any attention. In his 40s, Mencius left his hometown to travel to other states with his ideal of "benevolent governing", and the travel with his disciples lasted for more than twenty years.

　　As early as the reign of Duke Huan of Qi, Linzi, the capital of the State of Qi, had already set up Jixia Academy. They invited scholars of different philosophical schools to lecture and write, and to discuss political situation. Under the reign of Duke Wei of Qi, the schools were booming. Therefore, Mencius made Qi the first stop of his tour.

◎孟子不顾世风人言与匡章交友图
Mencius befriending Kuang Zhang

　　在齐国，孟子结识了一个"特别"的朋友——匡章。匡章的母亲因得罪丈夫，被丈夫杀死埋在马栈之下。匡章多次劝说父亲改葬母亲，父亲都不听，两人因此分开居住。齐国人都认为匡章不孝，孟子却知道匡章为母亲尽了心。后来，匡章赶走妻儿，不让他们照顾自己。因为匡章觉得父亲失去了天伦之乐，自己如果享受这种快乐就是不道德的，才赶走妻儿。因此，孟子十分敬重他，常与他讨论问题。匡父至死未原谅匡母，匡章尊重父亲，因此也就一直不敢违背父意改葬母亲。直到后来，他作为将军带兵拒秦，大胜而返，齐威王才为他改葬了母亲。

In the State of Qi, Mencius made a "special" friend — Kuang Zhang. Kuang Zhang's mother offended his father and was killed by the latter. His father buried his mother under the horse stack. Kuang Zhang tried to persuade his father to bury his mother elsewhere, but his father refused, so they two separated. The people of Qi regarded Kuang Zhang as an unfilial son, but Mencius understood that for his mother, Kuang Zhang tried his best. Afterwards, Kuang Zhang asked his wife and children to leave him, not allowing them to take care of him. And he though it was immoral to enjoy family happiness while his father lost his, so he did that to his wife and children. Mencius respected him for what he had done and had discussions with him over many issues. Kuang Zhang's father never forgave his mother even until his death. Kuang Zhang respected his father's will, and did not try to rebury his mother until he won a battle against the State of Qin. And Duke Wei of Qi reburied his mother for him.

◎孟子虽为卿不见用图
Mencius being neglected

君不乡道，不志于仁，而求富之，是富桀也。（《孟子·告子下》）

孟子到齐国后的很长一段时间里，都没有得到齐威王的重用，后来虽被拜为卿大夫，他的"仁政"主张却难容于齐国现行的法家政策之中，他常常为此感到忧虑。

Mencius had been in the State of Qi for a long time but he was not put in an important position. Though he was later promoted to be a minister, it was very difficult for the "benevolent government" he advocated to be integrated into existing legalist policy. Mencius was quite worried about this.

◎孟母述妇人之道图
Mother on women obedience

在彼者，皆我所不为也；在我者，皆古之制也，吾何畏彼哉？
（《孟子·尽心下》）

　　一日，孟子闲居在家，思索着自己的境遇，心中感慨，抚楹长叹。母亲闻声询问。孟子道："君子要从心所愿接受职位，不接受不正当的赏赐，不贪慕虚荣之禄，主张不被采纳就不进谏，采纳了不推行就不踏足朝廷。现在我的主张不被齐国国君采用，想要离开到别国去，念及母亲年迈，故而叹息。"

　　孟母告诉孟子："妇人之德在于料理家务，有三从之道：在家从父亲，出嫁从丈夫，夫死则从子。你已成人，只管按自己的意愿行事，我虽然年老，自会遵从。"但顾及母亲身体，孟子并未轻易远行。

　　One day, Mencius stayed at home. He was thinking about his circumstances and sighed. Hearing that, his mother asked why. Mencius said, "A gentleman should hold a post by following his heart. He should not accept reward he is not entitled to. He should not accept salary he does not deserve. If his advice is not accepted, he should offer no more. If his advice is adopted but not followed, he should not set his foot in the royal court. Now that my proposals are not accepted by the duke of Qi, I should leave elsewhere. But Mother is very old, and I cannot do that. That's why I sighed."

　　Mother told Mencius, "A woman's virtue lies in managing the household affairs and in three types of obedience: obedience to her father before marriage, and her husband during married life and her sons in widowhood. You are an adult now, and you just have to do whatever you feel like doing. I will obey even though I'm old." Considering Mother's health, Mencius did not travel far.

◎孟子父母合葬处

三年之丧　孔子提倡的丧礼习俗，也是中国古代丧服礼制中丧期最长的一种：父母去世，子女需守丧三年，期间的服饰、言容、居处、娱乐、饮食等都有特殊规定，甚至不能外出工作。

◎孟子丧母行孝图
Mencius in mourning

第二年，孟母离世。孟子想到母亲对自己的养育与教诲，悲痛不已，亲自为母亲料理丧事。他为母亲缝制了精美的衣衾，用上好木料制作了棺椁，把母亲送回鲁国归葬祖坟。按照卿大夫的礼制，孟子用五个鼎供奉了羊、猪、切肉、鱼和腊肉，并守孝三年。

When Mother passed away, thinking of Mother's rearing and teaching, Mencius felt so grieved over her death. He arranged everything for Mother's funeral. He had beautiful clothes and quilts sewed, the coffin of best quality made, and he buried her in the ancestral cemetery in the State of Lu. He offered in five vessels sacrifices of lamb, pig, chopped meat, fish and preserved meat according to the rituals a minister could practice. Then Mencius observed three-year mourning for his mother.

◎孟子之宋万章问政图
Wan Zhang consulting Mencius

*苟行王政，四海之内皆举首而望之，欲以为君；齐、楚虽大，何畏焉？（《孟子·滕文公下》）*

　　算起来，孟子到齐国已有六七年的时间，对齐威王已没有了期待。母亲离世后，再无牵挂的孟子选择了离开，到他国追寻梦想。时正值宋偃王当政，欲实施仁政，孟子便决定去宋国。

　　万章问孟子："宋这样的小国想实行仁政，齐、楚两个大国若因此而讨厌它，出兵攻击，该怎么办呢？"孟子却自信满满，笑答："宋国虽小，只要国君能真正实行仁政，天下人就会翘首期盼并拥戴他做君王，齐、楚纵然强大，又有什么好怕的呢？"

　　Mencius had been in the State of Qi for about six or seven years, and he felt he could expect nothing of Duke Wei of Qi. After Mother passed away, Mencius had nothing to worry about. He decided to leave for other states to pursue his ambition. Duke Yan of Song just claimed the crown, and wanted to practice benevolent governing. Mencius thus went to the State of Song.

　　Wan Zhang, a disciple of Mencius, asked him, "Song is such a small state. If this state practices benevolent governing, big states such as Qi and Chu would hate it and launch attacks against it. What can Song do?" Mencius smiled in confidence, "If a small state like Song can really practice benevolent governing, the whole world will be very happy to support their king. Though Qi and Chu are stronger states, what is Song scared of ?"

◎孟子辞宋归邹图

Mencius returning to Zou from Song

但是，到宋国后不久，孟子就发现，宋王身边贤人太少。有德之人刚刚离开，小人们就都围了上来，宋王身处其间，又能和谁一起做"好事"呢？要在这里推行仁政，就像楚大夫想让儿子学好齐国话，却天天被身边的楚国人影响一样，太难了。无奈之下，孟子只得向宋王请辞，宋王赠送他 70 镒金作为路费。路过薛国时，薛王又馈赠孟子 50 镒金，让他购买防身兵器。一路辗转，年逾五旬的孟子回到了阔别已久的家乡。

When arriving at Song, Mencius soon found that there were few virtuous people around the duke of Song. Righteous people just left, then crafty sycophants swarmed and gathered around the duke. Surrounded by these people, how was it possible for the duke to do something good? To promote benevolent governing here was as hard as learning to speak Qi dialect in a group of Chu people. In desperation, Mencius asked to leave. The duke of Song gave him 70 *yi* (a weight unit in ancient China) of gold as his traveling expenses. When Mencius passed by the State of Xue, the duke of Xue gave him 50 *yi* gold so that he could buy some weapons to protect himself. After experiencing many troubles, the 50-year-old Mencius finally came back home.

◎孟子居邹图
Mencius in Zou

孟子弟子众多，有乐正克、公孙丑、万章、公都子、陈臻、
充虞、咸丘蒙、陈代、彭更、屋庐连、桃应、徐辟、孟仲子等。

　　十多年过去了，回到家乡的孟子望着双亲已然不
在的家，想着自己仍未实现的理想，不免黯然。好在此
时他已桃李满天下，自有弟子追随左右。还有那些只
随孟子学习了一段时间便离开、散于各国的弟子，也
时常回来向他请教。

　　More than 10 years had passed when Mencius came back
home. Seeing the house without parents and thinking about his
unfulfilled ambition, Mencius felt so depressed. Fortunately,
Mencius now had a lot of disciples following him. Though some
persons left him after a period of learning, they would come
back to consult him from time to time.

◎屋庐连赴邹问礼与食图
Wulu Lian consulting about etiquette and dining

一个任国人问屋庐连："礼和食哪个重要？"屋庐连答："礼重要。"那人又问："如果按礼节去找吃的，就会饿死；不按礼节去找就会得到，还依礼行事吗？"屋庐连茫然不知如何作答。第二天，他专程赶赴邹国向老师请教。孟子教导他说："如不去衡量基础的高度，就直接拿双方的末端来比的话，一寸长的木块也能比尖顶高楼更高。金子比羽毛重，但三钱多的金子跟一整车的羽毛哪个重？很多状况是没有标准答案的，人必须学会分辨本末轻重。"

A man from the State of Ren asked Wulu Lian, "Which is more important, etiquette or dining?" Wulu Lian replied, "Etiquette." The man asked again, "If someone looks for something to eat by following the etiquette, he will be starved to death; if he does not, he will find something. In that case, does he still have to obey the etiquette?" Wulu Lian was left speechless. Wulu Lian went to the State of Zou to consult his master the very next day. Mencius explained to him, "If we do not consider the foundation, the end of a piece of wood could be higher than the top of a building. Gold is heavier than feather. But is it possible that three *qian* (a weight unit in ancient China) of gold is heavier than a cartful of feather? There are no standard answers for many situations. Thus, one has to learn to tell what more important is."

◎孟子闻乐正克为政图
Mencius feeling proud of Yuezheng Ke

孟子曰："人皆有不忍人之心。先王有不忍人之心，斯有
不忍人之政矣。以不忍人之心，行不忍人之政，治天下可
运之掌上。"（《孟子·公孙丑上》）

　　乐正克因其善良、真诚而深受孟子喜爱。听说鲁平公有意让他治理国政，孟子高兴得睡不着觉。

　　公孙丑问："乐正克刚强吗？有谋略吗？见多识广吗？"孟子说："都不是，他只是喜欢听取善言。"公

　　孙丑问："这样就够了吗？"孟子道："当然。如果乐于听取善言，天下之人都会不远千里赶来把善言告诉他，他就会不断成长。集天下之善，治国又有何难？"

Mencius liked kind-hearted and sincere Yuezheng Ke. Learning that Duke Ping of Lu had the intention to put Yuezheng Ke in charge of the state, Mencius was too excited to sleep.

Gongsun Chou asked, "Is Yuezheng Ke strong-willed? Is he resourceful or well-informed?" Mencius said, "Neither. But he is willing to listen to different opinions." "Is that enough?"

Gongsun Chou asked again. Mencius explained, "Of course. If Yuezheng Ke is willing to listen to others, people will come all the way to share with him their advice, and Yuezheng Ke will benefit and grow. With all the good advice, what could be the difficulty of ruling a state?"

孟子画传
MENCIUS

◎臧仓阻鲁平公访孟子图

Zang Cang dissuading Duke Ping of Lu from meeting Mencius

　　乐正克执政后，向鲁平公推荐了自己的老师。这天，鲁平公正要出门，宠臣臧仓迎了上来："往常您出外都先把地点告诉有司，今天车马都备好了，有司却不知道您要去哪里，特来请示。"鲁平公答："去拜访孟子。"臧仓阻止道："您怎么能屈尊，去拜访一个普通人呢？孟子是贤德之人吗？他为母亲办的丧礼规模远远超过父亲的葬礼，这是贤者所为吗？国君千万不要去见他。"鲁平公听信了臧仓的话，不再去拜见孟子。

　　Yuezheng Ke recommended his master to Duke Ping of Lu. One day when Duke Ping of Lu was leaving, his favorite vassal Zang Cang greeted him, saying, "You usually tell the driver where you are going. But today when the driver got the coach ready, he did not know where he should head for, and he begged for instructions." Duke Ping of Lu replied, "I'm going to visit Mencius." Zang Cang stopped him by saying, "How could you allow yourself to visit such an ordinary person? Is Mencius a virtuous person? He was very extravagant on his mother's funeral and spent more money than on his father's. Is this something a virtuous person is supposed to do? Your Majesty should not visit him." Duke Ping of Lu took in what Zang Cang said, and did not visit Mencius.

◎孟子叹不遇鲁侯天也图
Mencius lamenting his not meeting Duke Ping

孟子曰："欲贵者，人之同心也。人人有贵于己者，弗思耳矣。
人之所贵者，非良贵也。赵孟之所贵，赵孟能贱之。"（《孟
子·告子上》）

　　乐正克谒见鲁平公，问他为什么没去见孟子。鲁
平公把臧仓的话告诉了他。乐正克解释道："孟子之
前为士，以三鼎拜祭父亲；后为卿大夫，改用五鼎拜祭
母亲，没有错呀。"鲁平公说："我说的是棺椁衣物的
华美。"乐正克又答："这只是前后贫富不同的缘故。"
之后，乐正克把鲁平公要来拜访却被阻止的事告诉了
孟子。孟子听后感慨："来与不来，岂是人力所能左右。
是上天不让我与鲁侯相遇啊，不是小小宠臣所能阻止
的啊！"

　　Yuezheng Ke requested an audience with Duke Ping of
Lu and asked why he hadn't gone to see Mencius. Duke Ping
repeated what Zang Cang said. Yuezheng Ke explained to him,
"Mencius used to be an official, so he offered sacrifice in three
vessels, but later he was a minister, so he offered sacrifice in five
vessels. There is nothing wrong with him." Duke Ping said, "How
about the expensive coffin and sumptuous clothes?" Yuezheng
Ke answered, "That's because different situations." Yuezheng Ke
told Mencius why Duke Ping had not paid him a visit. Mencius
sighed, "No one can manipulate his coming or not. He is not
meant to meet me. A vassal is unable to stop him."

◎滕文公问孟子葬礼图
Duke Wen of Teng consulting Mencius for funeral

曾子曰：“生，事之以礼；死，葬之以礼，祭之以礼，可谓孝矣。”（《孟子·滕文公上》）

滕文公还是太子的时候，曾慕名拜访了孟子两次，听他讲尧舜之事及人性本善的道理。孟子回到邹国后，滕文公派然友两次询问父亲葬礼的礼仪。因此，孟子认为滕文公非常懂礼。滕文公即位后，便聘请孟子到滕国来，给他安排上等的馆舍，出门常有几十辆车、好几百人跟随。

When Duke Wen of Teng was still a prince, he visited Mencius twice out of admiration. He listened attentively to what Mencius said about Emperor Yao and Shun, and what he commented on human nature. When Mencius returned to the State of Zou, Duke Wen of Teng sent Ran You, his teacher, to consult Mencius twice about his father's funeral. Mencius believed that Duke Wen of Teng observed rituals. After Duke Wen became the ruler, he invited Mencius to the State of Teng, and hosted him in a very good guesthouse. When Mencius traveled, there usually came along with dozens of carriages and hundreds of entourages.

## ◎孟子与滕文公论为国图
Mencius on ruling a country

*民之为道也，有恒产者有恒心，无恒产者无恒心。（《孟子·滕文公上》）*

　　滕文公很乐意听取孟子的意见，向他请教如何治国。孟子建议："实行井田制，给百姓固定的产业，让他们安心；征收税赋不宜太繁重，百姓自会富足；兴办学校，传授伦理道德，百姓就会互相关爱、拥戴国君；让百姓服役，应错开农忙时节，不影响生产，国家自然稳定富强。"

　　但滕国是个方圆只有五十里的小国，日日担心的就是外敌入侵，只能在大国的夹缝中求生存，以免遭灭国之祸。邻国薛国被灭，齐国派兵来加固城池，滕文公闻之，如临大敌。因此，孟子所言是不符合当时的治国形势的。

Duke Wen of Teng was very happy to hear what Mencius had to say about ruling a country. Mencius said, "If the nine-square field system is implemented, ordinary people will be allowed to have some property and also a sense of security; if less tax is levied, the society will prosper; if schools are set up to teach morality, people will help each other and love and support their king; if young men are enlisted in the slack season, farming will not be affected, and the country will be strong."

But Teng was a small state with an area of 50 *li*, and had to struggle for survival among big states. Its greatest concern was invasion. When the neighboring state Xue was conquered and Qi sent troops as garrison, Duke Wen of Teng was so scared. Therefore, what Mencius advised was not feasible.

墨家，战国诸子百家之一，由墨翟创立，主张"兼爱""尚贤""节葬""非攻""天志""明鬼"，在当时影响很大

　　虽然在滕国期间孟子的治国方案未能得到推行，但他的影响与名望却显著提高，一些学者常来与他探讨、辩论。墨者夷之求见孟子，孟子托病不见。夷之再次拜访，孟子道："墨家主张薄葬，夷之却厚葬自己的父母，这是用自己鄙薄的方式对待父母啊！"夷之辩道：

"古代君王爱护百姓如婴儿，就指人对人的爱并无亲疏厚薄之别。"孟子道："夷之把恻隐之心当作爱无差等。但人的根源只有一个，就是自己的父母。"夷子听后怅然，自言："受教了。"

◎孟子与墨者夷之论葬图
Mencius discussing funeral with a Mohist

When Mencius was in the State of Teng, his way of governing a country did not get adopted, but his influence and reputation got enhanced. Some scholars came to have discussions with him. A Mohist scholar Yi Zhi requested an audience with Mencius, but Mencius pleaded sickness. Yi Zhi paid a visit for the second time. Mencius said, "Mohists encourage simple funeral, but Yi Zhi buried his parents in a grand way that he himself disapproves of." Yi Zhi argued, "A king in ancient time loves his people in the same way as he loves an infant. That means there should be no distinction in love." Mencius said, "Yi Zhi confused love with compassion. But man has only one source, and that is his parents." Learning that, Yi Zhi muttered in a depressed way, "I got it."

◎农家许行之滕图
Xu Xing of the Agriculturist school in Teng

孟子曰："尽信书，则不如无书。吾于武成，取二三策而已矣。
仁人无敌于天下，以至仁伐至不仁，而何其血之流杵也？"
（《孟子·尽心下》）

农家的许行率弟子数十人自楚国来到滕国，他们身穿粗麻衣服，以编草鞋、织席子为生。儒家陈良的门徒陈相和他的弟弟也背着农具从宋国来到滕国。陈相见到许行后非常高兴，尽弃之前所学，改向许行学习。

Xu Xing of the Agriculturist school went to the State of Teng from the State of Chu. He and his disciples were in coarse linen clothes, and they made their livings by weaving straw sandals and mats. Chen Xiang, a disciple of Chen Liang from Confucian school together with his younger brother also came to Teng from the State of Song with farm tools on their backs. Chen Xiang was very happy to see Xu Xing, and learned from Xu Xing as if he had never learned anything before.

◎孟子与陈相辩论图
Mencius debating with Chen Xiang

公都子曰："外人皆称夫子好辩，敢问何也？" 孟子曰："予
岂好辩哉？予不得已也！"（《孟子·滕文公下》）

　　许行的新门徒陈相来见孟子，转述许行的话："滕
国国君不与百姓一起耕种养活自己，还要让百姓供养，
怎么算得上贤明呢？"孟子反问："许行的帽子是自己
织的吗？烧饭的锅、耕田的铁器都是自己制作的吗？"
陈相说："不是。"孟子讲道："社会一定要有分工，
有人劳心，有人劳力。如果一定要亲自制作然后使用，
天下人都将疲于奔命。市场上的商品有普通的，也有
精美的。如果粗糙的鞋子和精致的鞋子一样的价钱，
谁还会做精致的鞋子，社会还会有进步吗？"

　　Chen Xiang came to see Mencius, and told him what Xu
Xing had said, "The duke of Teng does not plough and sow as
his people do to support himself, how can he be called a virtuous
duke?" Mencius asked, "Did Xu Xing weave his own hat? Did
he make his own cookers and farming tools?" Chen Xiang said,
"Of course not." Mencius said, "There exist some labor divisions
in the society. Some work more with their brains, some their
muscles. If people have to make everything for themselves, they
must be very tired with running different errands. There are both
ordinary and exquisite goods in the market. If a pair of shoddy
shoes asks for the same price as a pair of fancy shoes, who will
make the fancy? How can the society make progress?"

◎梁惠王郊迎邹衍图
Duke Hui of Liang greeting Zou Yan in the suburb

九流：儒家、道家、阴阳家、法家、名家、墨家、纵横家、杂家、农家。

梁国是战国时期的大国之一，为扩张疆土，长期与齐、秦、楚等国打仗。战争中，梁惠王不但丢失了城池，还失去了长子。晚年的梁惠王为了改善国家状况，用谦卑的礼仪、丰厚的待遇寻求贤能之人。

阴阳家邹衍曾是稷下名流，来到了梁国。梁惠王亲自到郊外迎接，以贵宾之礼待他。孟子于邹衍之后到达，却未受到如此待遇。

The State of Liang was once one of the strong states. To expand its borders, Liang was at war with the State of Qi, Qin and Chu for many years. In the war, Duke Hui of Liang not only lost many cities, but also his eldest son. When he was old, Duke Hui wanted to improve the situation. He invited the talented people and treated them with humble manner and generous offer.

Zou Yan, a representative of the Yin-Yang school and a famous scholar, came to Liang. Duke Hui went to the suburb to greet him, and treated him as a distinguished guest. Mencius arrived there later, but was not well received.

◎孟子为梁惠王论仁义图
Mencius discussing benevolence with Duke Hui

孟子曰："不仁而得国者，有之矣；不仁而得天下者，未之有也。"（《孟子·尽心下》）

梁惠王初见孟子，问："老先生，您不远千里而来，能给梁国带来什么利益呢？"

秉承孔子思想的孟子答道："您为什么一开口就说利益呢？只讲仁义就好了。关注利益的人不会满足。如果全国上下互相争夺利益，国家就会陷入危险之中，士大夫不夺取国君的产业不会罢休。只有讲仁德、重义行的人才不会丢弃父母、轻慢君王。"

Duke Hui asked Mencius when he met him for the first time, "My good man, you came all the way to see me, do you have something with which I can profit my kingdom?"

Mencius who adhered to Confucianism replied, "Why do you talk about profits when you open your mouth? What I have is benevolence. That's all. He who only cares about his profits is insatiable. If everyone across the country fights for their own profits, they will only put the country in danger; ministers will never be satisfied until they take the power away from the king. Only those benevolent and righteous people will not desert their parents, and will not disrespect their king."

◎孟子论贤者之乐图
Mencius discussing happiness with Duke Hui

乐民之乐者，民亦乐其乐；忧民之忧者，民亦忧其忧。乐以
天下，忧以天下，然而不王者，未之有也。（《孟子·梁惠
王下》）

孟子去拜见梁惠王。梁惠王正立于池边，欣赏园中景致：鸿雁翱翔于林上，麋鹿觅食在水边，一切是那么的宁静祥和。

看到孟子，梁惠王问："古代贤者也享受这种快乐吗？"孟子答道："周文王修筑灵台、灵沼，百姓欢心，鸢飞鱼跃；夏桀纵有高台深池，百姓却恨不得与他同归于尽。只有有德之人才能享受这种快乐啊！"

Mencius visited Duke Hui of Liang. Duke Hui was standing beside a pond, admiring the peaceful and beautiful scenery in the garden: Swan geese were hovering over the woods; elks were grazing by the pond.

Seeing Mencius, Duke Hui asked, "Could sages in the ancient time also enjoy such peace and beauty?" Mencius said,

"King Wen of Zhou built temples and ponds. His people were happy; birds flew freely, and fish swam leisurely. Jie, the king of Xia Dynasty, also built temples and ponds, but his people hated him and wanted him to die. Only those virtuous people can enjoy the peace and happiness."

◎梁惠王辞世图
Duke Hui passing away

今王发政施仁，使天下仕者皆欲立于王之朝，耕者皆欲耕于王之野，商贾皆欲藏于王之市，行旅皆欲出于王之涂，天下之欲疾其君者皆欲赴愬于王。其若是，孰能御之？（《孟子·梁惠王上》）

　　对于自己在战争中的失败，梁惠王一直耿耿于怀："想我梁国也曾是数一数二的大国，而我却接连败于齐、秦、楚，太屈辱了，如何为战死之人报仇雪恨呢？"

　　孟子进谏："大王若对百姓实施仁政，少用刑罚，减轻赋税；让年轻人学习孝悌忠信，在家侍奉父兄，在外尊重长上，他们即使拿着木棍也能打败齐、楚。古语称这为'仁者无敌'。"

　　多次交谈之后，梁惠王对孟子钦佩不已。但上天又一次捉弄了孟子，孟子到梁国的第二年，惠王就去世了。

Duke Hui felt very upset about his loss in the war all day long, "We were once a powerful state, but I lost battles time and time again to the State of Qi, Qin and Chu. It is really humiliating. What can I do to take revenge for the soldiers who have fought to death?"

Mencius advised, "Your Majesty should practice benevolent governing, enforce less frequently penalty, and levy less tax. If Your Majesty encourages young people to learn filial piety, they would be able to serve their father and brother at home and respect seniors and superiors when they go out, and they would defeat Qi and Chu even with sticks in their hands. That's what 'benevolence is insurmountable' meant in the ancient time'."

Duke Hui admired Mencius very much after many such discussions. But Fortune did not play favorites with Mencius once again, Duke Hui died the very next year after Mencius came to Liang.

◎孟子遇齐王之子图
Mencius meeting Duke Xuan of Qi

可以仕则仕，可以止则止，可以久则久，可以速则速：孔子也。
（《孟子·公孙丑上》）

梁惠王之子襄王即位，孟子谒见襄王。出宫后，孟子叹道："远远望去，不像个国君的样子；走近了，也看不到威严所在。与我交流，更是前言不搭后语。"孟子感到自己再待在梁国已毫无益处。

此时，正逢齐威王去世，其子宣王继位，实施新政。

孟子决定离开梁国再次赴齐。经过范邑时，恰巧碰到齐宣王在外巡视，远远望去颇具王者风范，孟子不禁感叹："居住环境改变气度，饮食奉养影响体态，环境的影响真大啊！"

Duke Xiang succeeded his father Duke Hui. Mencius had an audience with him. Mencius sighed after the meeting, "When I saw him at a distance, he did not have the bearing of a ruler of the state; when I approached him, I did not see his authority; when I talked with him, he was unable to express himself well." Mencius thought he would get nowhere if he still stayed in Liang.

Duke Wei of Qi also passed away. His son Duke Xuan took his place and implemented new policy. Mencius decided to leave the State of Liang for the State of Qi for the second time.Passing by Fan County, Mencius happened to meet Duke Xuan when the duke was on his inspection tour. Mencius was impressed by Duke Xuan's royal bearing. Mencius said, "Living environment can impact his bearing and his daily life can influence his deportment. Environment is not to be taken lightly."

◎孟子将朝齐王图
Mencius going to meet the duke of Qi

君之视臣如手足，则臣视君如腹心；君之视臣如犬马，则臣视君如国人；君之视臣如土芥，则臣视君如寇雠。（《孟子·离娄下》）

　　孟子的知名度与初次来齐时已不可同日而语。齐宣王对他甚是好奇，派人窥探他的日常起居，想看看他究竟和别人有什么不同。孟子得知后，笑道："能有什么不一样呢？即使是尧、舜，也和一般人没什么区别啊！"

　　这天，孟子正要去觐见齐宣王。宣王派使者传信："我原想来看望您的，不巧着了凉，不能吹风。如果您来朝见，我就临朝办公。不知您肯来见我吗？"孟子听后，对使者说："不幸得很，我也生病了，没办法上朝。"

Mencius was more famous than the first time when he came to the State of Qi. Duke Xuan was very curious about him, sending someone to check out his daily life to see if there was something unusual about him. Mencius laughed, "What could be the differences? Even Yao and Shun did not act differently from ordinary people."

One day, Mencius was going to request an audience with Duke Xuan. But the duke had a message delivered, "I wanted to see you, but unfortunately I caught a cold and could not brave the weather. If you come to see me, I will come to the court. Are you willing to come?" Mencius said to the messenger, "Unfortunately, I'm sick, too. I cannot go to the court."

◎齐王使人问孟子疾图
Duke asking about Mencius' illness

第二天,孟子要去东郭大夫家吊丧。公孙丑劝他说:"您昨天才托词有病谢绝宣王的召见,今天就去吊丧,不太好吧。"孟子道:"昨天生病,今天却好了,为什么不能去吊丧呢?"

孟子刚出门,齐王就派人来探病,还有医生同行。

孟仲子告诉使者:"昨天接到大王命令,他正好生病不能前去。今天病稍好,他就赶紧上朝去了,不知道现在到了没有?"

使者一离开,孟仲子就急忙派人到孟子回家的路上拦阻他,告诉他:"你千万不要回家,赶紧上朝去吧。"

The next day, Mencius was going to the Dongguos to attend mourning service. His disciple Gongsun Chou persuaded, "You declined to see the Duke Xuan by making the excuse of sickness yesterday, but you are going to mourn somebody today. Is it proper?" Mencius said, "I was ill yesterday, but I'm better today. Why cannot I go?"

Duke Xuan sent a messenger and a doctor to visit Mencius when he just left. Mengzhong Zi, one of Mencius' disciples, told the messenger, "Mencius was too sick to go yesterday. He is feeling better today, and he is hurrying to the court. Is he there yet?"

When the messenger left, Mengzhong Zi sent several people to stop Mencius on his way home, and asked him to go the court directly.

◎孟府大门

欲见贤人而不以其道，犹欲其入而闭之门也。夫义，路也；礼，门也。惟君子能由是路，出入是门也。（《孟子·万章下》）

◎孟子为景丑论君使臣之道图

## Mencius on the interaction between a king and his ministers

　　孟子没办法，只得躲到景丑的家里去住宿。景丑不明白，问道："我见大王对您很是敬重，却没看见您怎么尊敬大王啊？"

　　孟子解释道："天下公认为尊贵的有三样：爵位、年龄、道德。在朝堂上，先论爵位；在乡里中，先论年龄；至于辅助君主、统治百姓自然以道德为最上。齐王怎能凭他的爵位轻视我的年龄和道德呢？所以想要有大作为的君主，必定有他不能召见的臣子，若有事要商量，那就亲自前去请教。如果他不能诚心实意地崇尚道德、喜爱仁义，就不值得同他一起干事。"

　　Mencius had no choice but to hide in the home of Jing Chou's. Jing Chou could not understand why Mencius did so, and asked, "It seems to me that Duke Xuan showed great respect to you, but you did not do the same to him."

　　Mencius explained, "It is widely acknowledged that we should pay respect to three things: the rank of nobility, age and virtue. In a royal court, rank matters; in a village, age matters; in helping a ruler to govern a country, virtue matters. How can a duke place his title above my age and virtue and disrespect me? A ruler cannot summon his ministers at will. If the ruler has something to consult, he needs to visit the minister, and the minister is willing to support him, and then he could conquer the world without much difficulty."

◎孟子雪宫再论贤者之乐图
Mencius discussing happiness with Duke Xuan

◎孟子雪宫再论贤者之乐图
Mencius discussing happiness with Duke Xuan

临淄郊外有处离宫叫雪宫，亭台楼阁装饰华丽，园中豢养着各种珍禽异兽。宣王召孟子至此问道："贤者也有这种快乐吗？"孟子答："有。如果没有，他们就会抱怨君主。得不到就抱怨君主，不对；但作为君主却不与民同乐，更不对。与天下人同忧同乐，还不能称王，是不曾有过的。"

宣王又问："听说周文王的园林纵横各七十里，是真的吗？"孟子答："史书是这样记载的。"宣王不禁问道："我的园林纵横才各四十里，怎么百姓都觉得大呢？"孟子说："文王园林虽大，却是与百姓一起享用的，割草砍柴、打鸟捕兔的人都能进入。而在您的园林中，杀了只麋鹿就跟犯了杀人的罪一样，百姓怎么能觉得不大呢？"

Duke Xuan had a holiday residence in the suburb in Linzi called "Snow Palace". The palace was sumptuously decorated, and many rare species of animals were kept there. The duke summoned Mencius here and asked, "Can sages feel the same happiness?" Mencius said, "Yes. If they don't, they will complain about the ruler. It is wrong for them to complain about something they cannot get. But it is worse if their ruler cannot let his people feel the happiness. I have never heard that a ruler could not conquer the world when he shares with people his happiness."

Duke Xuan asked again, "It is said that the garden of King Wen of Zhou has an area as big as 70 *li*. Is it true?"

Mencius answered, "It is so, according to the historical record."

"But mine is only 40 *li*. Why my people think it is very big?" asked the duke again.

"Though the garden of King Wen was very big, he shared with his people. Farmers and hunters could all go into. But in your garden, shooting an elk is just as unforgivable as killing a man. Small wonder that your people think it is too big!"

◎孟子出吊于滕图
Mencius at mourning service

　　滕文公逝世，齐宣王派孟子去吊丧，盖邑大夫王
驩（字子敖）为副使同行。一路上，王驩早晚都要来见
孟子，但在往返齐国与滕国的路上，孟子却不曾和他
谈起过出使的事情。公孙丑不解，便问孟子。孟子说：
"这事既然有人在办了，我还要说什么呢？"

　　齐国大夫公行子为儿子办丧事，王驩也去吊唁。
他一进门，大家都去跟他寒暄，孟子却不理他。王驩
很不高兴，说道："各位大夫都来跟我说话，只有孟子
怠慢我啊。"孟子听到后说："依礼，在朝堂上不能越
过位置交谈，不能跨过台阶作揖。我以礼相待，子敖
却认为我怠慢了他，不是很奇怪吗？"

　　When Duke Wen of Teng passed away, Duke Xuan of Qi
sent Mencius to attend the mourning service. A minister Wang
Huan came along as a deputy envoy. Mencius did not talk with
him about the mission. Gongsun Chou did not quite understand.
Mencius explained, "He is very dictatorial. What can I say with
him?"

　　Wang Huan also went to another mourning service.
Everyone went up to greet him except Mencius. Wang Huan
was offended, saying, "Every minister came over to talk to me,
only Mencius cold-shouldered me." Learning that, Mencius said,
"We are not supposed to talk across from where we are, and not
supposed to bow to each other on the stairs. I followed the rules,
but he thought I had neglected him. Is that odd?"

孟庙 又称亚圣庙，始建于北宋景佑四年（1037年），坐落在邹城市东北四基山西麓的孟子墓旁。北宋元丰年间，迁至邹县旧城东门外，后因频受水灾，于北宋宣和三年（1121年）迁至现址。孟庙规模仅次于孔庙，是国内稀存的宋元至明清时期的古建筑代表作品。孟庙为五进院落建筑，以主体建筑"亚圣殿"为中心，南北为一条中轴线，左右对称式配列。

◎齐将军匡章伐燕图
Kuang Zhang attacking Yan

公元前316年，燕王哙把王位让给了相国子之，从此不过问政事。第二年，燕国发生内乱。太子平与将军市被攻打子之，几个月没有成功，反被子之杀害。齐宣王想借机吞并燕国，于是派将军匡章伐燕，五十天就攻下了燕国国都，擒住了子之，将他砍死。

In 316 B. C., the duke of Yan, Ji Kuai, gave his crown to the prime minister Zi Zhi, and never bothered to get involved in the state affairs ever since. The next year, a rebellion broke out. Prince Ping and General Shi Bei launched attacks against Zi Zhi, but they were killed by Zi Zhi. Duke Xuan of Qi wanted to take this advantage to acquire the State of Yan. He sent General Kuang Zhang to attack Yan, and after only about fifty days, the capital of Yan fell. Zi Zhi was caught and chopped to death.

◎孟子止君取燕图
Mencius advising Duke Xuan

孟子曰："天时不如地利，地利不如人和。……得道者多助，
失道者寡助。寡助之至，亲戚畔之；多助之至，天下顺之。
以天下之所顺，攻亲戚之所畔，故君子有不战，战必胜矣。"
（《孟子·公孙丑下》）

　　胜利后，齐军在燕国的行径十分残暴：不仅滥杀
无辜，抢夺财物，还毁坏燕国宗庙祠堂。各路诸侯于
是商讨出兵救燕。宣王问孟子该如何是好。孟子劝齐
王下令严肃军纪，停止残害百姓、掠夺财物，与燕国
百姓商量选立新君，然后撤兵。但齐宣王并没有采纳
孟子的建议。两年后，燕国人在诸侯的帮助下拥立燕
昭王，反抗齐国，齐军大败而返。齐宣王慨叹："我愧
对孟子。"

　　After Qi troops conquered Yan, they slaughtered innocent
people and looted wantonly, and destroyed their ancestral
temples. Other states discussed the possibility of rescuing Yan.
Duke Xuan of Qi asked Mencius about what to do next. Mencius
advised imposing severe discipline on soldiers and stopping
killing and looting, and at the same time withdrawing the troops
after helping Yan select their new ruler. Duke Xuan did not
follow Mencius' advice. Two years later, Yan people crowned
Duke Zhao with the help of other dukes. They then attacked and
defeated Qi. Duke Xuan of Qi regretted by saying, "I feel so
ashamed to face Mencius."

◎孟子致为臣齐宣王就见图
Mencius resigning

富贵不能淫，贫贱不能移，威武不能屈，此之谓大丈夫。
（《孟子·滕文公下》）

齐宣王因自己未听孟子劝谏而惭愧，孟子则因齐王不纳己见而失望，君臣间产生嫌隙。孟子决定辞去卿位，离开齐国。宣王不舍，亲自去见孟子，挽留他。孟子只能回答："希望以后还能相见。"

过了几天，齐王对时子说："我想在国都给孟子一处房屋，以万钟粮食供养他的弟子，让我国的百姓有所效法。你何不替我去说说？"孟子听后，回复说："如果我想发财，何必辞掉十万钟的俸禄，却接受这一万钟的赏赐呢？"

Duke Xuan of Qi felt ashamed for not following the advice, and Mencius felt so disappointed about not being listened to. A rift developed between them two. Mencius decided to resign and leave the State of Qi. Duke Xuan tried to ask him to stay. Mencius replied, "Hope we can see each other in the future."

Several days later, the duke said to Shi Zi, "I want to build a house for Mencius in the capital, and provide for his disciples. And my ministers and people will learn from my example. Would you please pass this message on?" Mencius said, "If I wanted to become rich, why did I give up my generous salary for a meager reward?"

◎孟子去齐宿于昼图
Mencius staying in Zhou

孟子曰："鱼，我所欲也；熊掌，亦我所欲也。二者不可得兼，舍鱼而取熊掌者也。生，亦我所欲也；义，亦我所欲也，二者不可得兼，舍生而取义者也。"（《孟子·告子上》）

孟子离齐，在昼县过夜。有人想替齐王挽留孟子，他恭敬地坐着同孟子说话，孟子却不加理会，伏在靠几上睡起觉来。那人很不高兴："我先斋戒一天才敢来跟您说话,您却睡觉不听,以后再也不敢与您相见了。"孟子忙道："如果不能得到齐王的尊重、任用，只因齐王的供养而留下来，你让我这个老头如何自处呢？"

Mencius left the State of Qi and stayed in Zhou County for one night. Someone wanted to keep Mencius in Qi on the behalf of Duke Xuan. He spoke respectably to Mencius, but Mencius just turned a deaf ear to him and dozed off on an end table. That man was very unhappy, saying, "I had been on a one-day fast before I came to see you. But you fall into sleep and do not listen. I don't have the courage to see you again." Mencius explained, "If I stay because I'm provided, but not because I'm valued. What can I justify myself for?"

◎孟子浩然而去图
Mencius leaving Qi

孟子曰："天将降大任于是人也，必先苦其心志，劳其筋骨，饿其体肤，空乏其身，行拂乱其所为，所以动心忍性，曾益其所不能。……然后知生于忧患而死于安乐也。"（《孟子·告子下》）

孟子在昼县停留了三天，希望齐王改变态度召他回去，并重用自己，让齐国太平、天下太平。但齐王终究没有来，孟子无奈地踏上了归程。

路上，充虞见孟子不高兴，便问："从前您不是说'君子不怨天尤人'吗？"孟子道："此一时，彼一时。

历史上每五百年必定有圣君兴起，也会有辅佐他的贤臣。周朝至今已有七百年了，上天如果想让天下太平，当今之世，舍我其谁？"

带着无限的怅惘，孟子结束了游历生涯，回到故乡。齐国是孟子游说诸侯的起点，也成了终点。

Mencius stayed in Zhou County for three days, hoping Duke Xuan would change his mind, and assign him an important task to accomplish, so that the State of Qi and the rest of the world could be left at peace. But Duke Xuan did not come. Mencius reluctantly set foot on the return journey.

Seeing Mencius was upset, Chong Yu asked, "You once said 'Gentleman complains about nothing and blames no one'." Mencius replied, "Circumstances alter cases. For every five hundred years there emerges a great king, and also a wise minister to support him. It has been seven hundred years since Zhou Dynasty. If peace is meant to reign, I'm the one to make it happen."

Mencius ended his traveling in disappointment and returned to his hometown. Qi was the state where he started and ended his lobby.

孟子六十多岁以
后专心讲学与弟
子公孙丑、万章
等人编纂曾经
的辩难答问之言
著自己的思想留
于后世约公元前
二百八十九年
终年八十四岁
者与世长辞
但他的思想却影
响着整个中华
民族十且至于今
发邑年初秋
李子海意绘制
于兰海忠心斋
并海题记

《孟子》一书共有七篇，分别为《梁惠王》《公孙丑》《滕
文公》《离娄》《万章》《告子》《尽心》，每篇再分上下，
共计 14 部分。

六十多岁的孟子回到邹国后专心讲学，与弟子公
孙丑、万章等人编纂游历中的辩难答问之言，著《孟子》
七篇，将自己的思想留传后世。

公元前 289 年，周赧王二十六年十一月十五日，
这位伟大的儒者与世长辞，终年 84 岁，但他的思想却
影响着整个中华民族，直至今日。

◎孟子归邹著述讲学图
Mencius lecturing in Zou

In his sixties, Mencius came back to the State of Zou and devoted himself to lecturing and writing. Mencius and his disciples Gongsun Chou, Wan Zhang and others collected and compiled his witty answers to tricky questions into a seven-chapter book *Mencius*, through which his thoughts were passed down to generations.

In 289 B. C., the great thinker passed away at age of 84, but his influence upon the Chinese people is far-reaching.

　　孟子的学说是儒家文化的重要组成部分，在对儒家文化发展史的贡献上与孔子齐名，俗称"孔孟之道"。将这样一位伟大哲人的一生，用中国传统的绘画形式再现于世人，无疑对弘扬中华文化是一件好事，也是一项艰巨的任务。

　　上海作为现代中国画创作基地之一，人才辈出，而人物画创作又是海派绘画的特色组成部分。将海派绘画的特色在创作《孟子画传》的过程中加以表现，是我在创作中孜孜追求的目标。在创作时，我始终注意运用线条来支撑整个画面，辅以墨韵及色彩的渲染，争取做到雅俗共赏，因为这也是海派绘画的特色之一。

　　当我完成全部创作，一幅幅画稿呈现在面前时，我的喜悦之情难以用语言来描述。通过创作《孟子画传》，我仿佛走进了孟子的内心深处，与他进行着心灵的对话。我又一次系统地学习了孟子的儒家学说，感受到了中华文化的博大精深。

　　我要感谢我的夫人吴曼姑，她为我的创作做了大量的资料收集工作。我要感谢上海海派连环画中心、济南出版社，给我这样一个难能可贵的机会：以中国画的笔墨描绘中华文化先贤、普及中华传统文化！感谢为这本书的出版做出辛勤努力的编辑人员！谢谢你们！

癸巳年孟冬

# The Artist's Words

Mencius' philosophy is definitely an integral part of Confucianism, and his contribution to the Confucian culture is no less than Confucius himself. It is a challenging task to recapture the sage's life in traditional Chinese painting and spread Chinese culture.

As a base of modern Chinese painting, Shanghai has nurtured a great many talents and developed its Shanghai style of figure painting. How to incorporate Shanghai style in creating *Mencius* has always been my artistic pursuit. I sketched the contours of figures and nature to prop up the entire space, completing with coloring to suit both refined and popular tastes.

When I completed my creation, and when all the paintings were in front of me, my joy was beyond words. Through *Mencius*, I got a chance to have a dialogue with Mencius, and to study Confucian philosophy systemically, and I was awed by the profundity of traditional Chinese culture.

I want to express my gratitude to my wife Wu Mangu, who has done a great deal of material collection for me. My many thanks go to Shanghai City Animation Corporation and Jinan Publishing House, for allowing me the opportunity to represent sages in traditional Chinese painting and spreading traditional Chinese culture. My thanks also go to the editing staff for their hard work. Thank you all!

Li Weiding
November 2013

中国国家主席习近平在谈及中华文化时，深刻地指出：「中华优秀传统文化已经成为中华民族的基因，植根在中国人内心，潜移默化影响着中国人的思想方式和行为方式。」厚重、灿烂的中华传统文化，如何借由一种生动、直观、亲切的方式走进读者，尤其是海外读者的阅读视野中，一直是文化界关注、思索的问题。当《诸子百家国风画传》丛书带着「传承、创新、中国风」的鲜明印迹从上海出发，正是希望由此探索向世界传播、普及中国优秀传统文化的新方式和新渠道。

上海，作为国际文化大都市，通过源源不断地推出文化交流精品，成为海外读者了解中国、感受中国的一扇精彩窗口。发源于上海的连环画艺术，则以其浓郁、独特的中国韵味深受国内外读者的欢迎。两年前，以传承、振兴中国连环画艺术为主旨的上海海派连环画中心甫一成立，即在上海市政府新闻办的指导、创意下，联合发起策划一套以国风连环画为载体、契合「读图时代」特点的《诸子百家国风画传》丛书，并得到了国务院新闻办公室、中共上海市委宣传部的大力支持，以及山东、河南省政府新闻办和相关诸子故里的密切协作。

尤为可贵的是，国内著名国画家郭德福、李维定、赵明钧、邵家声、忻秉勇为淋漓再现智者先贤而实地采风、遍览典籍、泼墨挥毫，探寻中国文化符号世界化表达的崭新方式。画家们数易其稿，精益求精，创作出让人耳目一新、形神兼备的诸子形象。画传不仅选取诸子生平中最具典型意义的事件，还注意表现鲜有人关注的诸子日常生活。画传想让读者感知的不只是存在于文献、传说里的古之圣贤，更是身边熟悉亲切、可以答疑解惑的智者。

我们衷心希望，这套充满哲理智慧与中国艺术美质的丛书能够成为连接当代与中华传统的文化桥梁。希望中华文化的寻源之旅能让每一个中国人寻回精神归属，也让海外读者从另一蹊径了解中国文化之美。

《诸子百家国风画传》丛书编委会
二〇一四年九月

# Afterword

President Xi Jinping made an insightful comment in his talking about Chinese culture, "The excellent traditional Chinese culture has become our genes deeply rooted in our heart, entered into and colored our patterns in thinking and behaving." How the rich and brilliant Chinese culture could be presented in a vivid, visual and approachable form to the readers, especially overseas readers, has always been the concern of the cultural circle. When *The Pictorial Biographies of Great Thinkers* series with its distinguishing features of "inheritance, originality, and Chinese style" is setting sail from Shanghai, it is hoped to be a new means and a new channel explored for spreading, popularizing the excellent Chinese culture.

As an international cultural metropolis, Shanghai has created continuously first-class cultural exchange project and become a window through which overseas readers get to know and understand China. The comic book painting art originated in Shanghai has always been well accepted by readers home and abroad for its rich and unique Chinese style. Two years ago, not long after Shanghai Comic Book Center established to inherit and revive the comic painting art, under the guidance of Information Office of Shanghai Municipality, the Center created a series of comic book — *The Pictorial Biographies of Great Thinkers* to appeal to the "visual era". This innovative project is supported by The State Council Information Office and Publicity Ministry of Shanghai Municipal committee of CPC, and this project is also a close cooperation between Information Office of Shandong Provincial People's Government, Information Office of Henan Provincial People's Government and Confucius hometown.

What made this series particularly valuable is the research work the artists did. To represent thoroughly and faithfully the great thinkers, Mr. Guo Defu, Mr. Zhao Mingjun, Mr. Shao Jiasheng and Mr. Xin Bingyong, not only read extensively the classics but also conducted field work. They tried different means of expression and revised numerous times for a better unity of appearance and spirit of the thinkers. The episodes in the pictorial biographies reveal both the milestone events great thinkers experienced and their daily life that usually went unnoticed. The great thinkers in the pictorial biographies are no longer legendary figure in the literature, but amiable saints we can approach with our problems for a solution.

We sincerely hope that this series rich in philosophical wisdom and Chinese aestheticism could bridge the contemporary China and its traditional culture. We also hope that the exploration of Chinese culture will give every Chinese a sense of spiritual belonging, and provide an alternative for overseas readers to get to know the beauty of Chinese culture.

Editing Committee of *The Pictorial Biographies of Great Thinkers*
September 2014